Campfire Cooking

Printed in the United States of America
by G&R Publishing Co.

Published By:

507 Industrial Street
Waverly, IA 50677

ISBN-13: 978-1-56383-192-8
ISBN-10: 1-56383-192-6
Item #7005

Table of Contents

On a Stick

Donut Snakes

Makes 8 servings

1 tube of 8 refrigerated biscuits   **Cinnamon and sugar mixture**
¼ C. butter, melted

Build a campfire. Unroll each biscuit and shape into a long strip. Wrap each biscuit around a long clean stick or long metal skewer. Hold sticks so biscuits are about 6" to 10" above hot coals. When biscuits are browned, push biscuits off sticks and onto a plate. Brush biscuits with melted butter and sprinkle generously with cinnamon and sugar mixture.

Equipment needed:
matches
long pointed sticks or skewers
plate
basting brush

Quick tip:
Prepare cinnamon and sugar mixture at home by combining 2 tablespoons sugar and 1 teaspoon cinnamon. Pack in an airtight container until ready to prepare recipe.

Yummy Breakfast Bag

Makes 1 serving

1 to 2 slices bacon   **1 to 2 eggs**
1 C. frozen hash browns, thawed

Build a simmering campfire. In a lunch-sized brown paper bag, place bacon slices and thawed hash browns. Crack eggs into bag. Fold paper bag down, leaving 3" of space above food. Insert a pointed stick through the folded part of the bag. Hold stick so bag hangs about 4" to 5" above hot coals. Cook for about 8 to 10 minutes, being careful not to let the bag catch on fire. Remove bag from heat and, using an oven mitt, fold open to check that eggs have been cooked throughout. If eggs have not completely cooked, refold paper bag and hold over hot coals for an additional 2 to 3 minutes. Fold down paper bag and eat breakfast directly from bag.

Equipment needed:
matches
lunch-sized brown paper bag
long pointed stick
oven mitt
fork

Hawaiian Roasts

Makes 4 servings

4 to 6 hot dogs, cut into pieces
1 (20 oz.) can pineapple
  chunks, drained

Build a campfire. Slide hot dog pieces and pineapple chunks onto 4 pointed sticks. Hold sticks about 8" to 10" above hot coals. Cook until hot dogs are heated throughout, about 5 to 8 minutes.

Equipment needed:
matches
can opener
4 long pointed sticks

Little Weiner Kabobs

Makes 4 servings

**1 pkg. Hillshire Farm
little smokies**
4 dill pickles, cut into ¾" pieces
1 pint cherry tomatoes
**1 (4 oz.) can button
mushrooms, drained**

**15 large pimiento-stuffed
green olives**
**1 green bell pepper, cut
into ¾" squares**

Build a campfire. Slide little smokies, pickle pieces, cherry tomatoes, button mushrooms, green olives and green bell pepper squares onto 4 pointed sticks. Hold sticks about 8" to 10" above hot coals. Cook until little smokies are heated throughout, about 5 to 8 minutes.

Equipment needed:
matches
sharp knife
can opener
4 long pointed sticks

Toasted Wacky Taffies

Makes 6 servings

6 wrapped caramel squares   **12 Ritz crackers**

Build a campfire. Unwrap caramel squares and insert one caramel onto the end of a pointed stick. Hold stick so caramel is about 12" to 15" above hot coals. Toast caramel over campfire just until softened, being careful not to melt caramel completely. Place one caramel between two Ritz crackers to make a sandwich. Repeat with remaining ingredients.

Equipment needed:
matches
long pointed stick

S'mores

Makes 1 serving

1 marshmallow   **½ Hershey's chocolate bar**
1 graham cracker

   Build a campfire. Insert marshmallow onto the end of a pointed stick. Hold stick so marshmallow is about 12" to 15" above hot coals. Toast marshmallow over campfire to desired doneness. Break graham cracker in half and place chocolate bar half on one of the crackers. Place toasted marshmallow between crackers to make a sandwich.

Equipment needed:
matches
long pointed stick

Sailor S'mores

Makes 1 serving

1 marshmallow　　　　　　**¼ Hershey's chocolate bar**
Creamy peanut butter　　　**2 saltine crackers**

　　Build a campfire. Insert marshmallow onto the end of a pointed stick. Hold stick so marshmallow is about 12" to 15" above hot coals. Toast marshmallow over campfire to desired doneness. Spread peanut butter onto one side of each saltine cracker and place chocolate bar piece on one of the saltines. Place toasted marshmallow between saltines to make a sandwich.

Equipment needed:
matches
knife
long pointed stick

In a Pie Iron

Portabella Melt

Makes 1 serving

1 large portabella   **1 to 2 slices mozzarella cheese**
mushroom cap

Build a flaming campfire. Generously grease both sides of the pie iron with non-stick cooking spray. Place portabella mushroom cap on one side and close iron. Hold pie iron over the fire, turning occasionally. Don't worry about overcooking. Open pie iron and place mozzarella cheese inside mushroom cap. Close iron and hold over flames for an additional 2 to 3 minutes, until cheese is melted. Remove iron from fire and open carefully with a hot pad or oven mitt.

Equipment needed:
matches
non-stick cooking spray
pie iron
hot pad or oven mitt

Hash Brown Pie

Makes 1 serving

1 C. frozen hash browns, thawed
½ C. chopped onions

1 tsp. garlic salt
Pepper to taste

Build a flaming campfire. Generously grease both sides of the pie iron with non-stick cooking spray. In a medium bowl, combine thawed hash browns, chopped onions and garlic salt. Mix well and season with pepper to taste. Pat hash browns mixture into a square and set on one side of the pie iron. Close iron and hold over flames for 8 to 10 minutes. Remove iron from fire and open carefully with a hot pad or oven mitt.

Equipment needed:
matches
sharp knife
non-stick cooking spray
medium bowl
spoon
pie iron
hot pad or oven mitt

Cinnamon or Garlic Biscuits

Makes 8 servings

1 tube of 8 buttermilk biscuits
2 T. butter, melted

Cinnamon and sugar mixture
OR 2 tsp. garlic salt

Build a flaming campfire. Generously grease both sides of the pie iron with non-stick cooking spray. Separate tube into individual biscuits. Roll each biscuit into a ball. Place either cinnamon and sugar mixture or garlic salt in a shallow bowl. Brush biscuits with melted butter and then roll in either cinnamon and sugar mixture or garlic salt. Place one biscuit ball on pie iron. Close iron and hold over flames for about 5 minutes, or until biscuit is golden brown. Remove iron from fire and open carefully with a hot pad or oven mitt. Repeat with remaining ingredients.

Equipment needed:
matches
non-stick cooking spray
shallow bowl
basting brush
pie iron
hot pad or oven mitt

Quick tip:
Prepare cinnamon and sugar mixture at home by combining 2 tablespoons sugar and 1 teaspoon cinnamon. Pack in an airtight container until ready to prepare recipe.

Breakfast Egg & Sausage Muffins

Makes 8 servings

8 English muffins, split in half
1 lb. sausage patties
8 to 10 eggs, scrambled and cooked

½ C. shredded cheese, any kind
Salt and pepper to taste

Build a flaming campfire. Generously grease both sides of the pie iron with non-stick cooking spray. Place one English muffin half on each side of a pie iron. Place 1 sausage patty, a little of the precooked scrambled eggs and 1 tablespoon shredded cheese on one English muffin half. Sprinkle with salt and pepper to taste. Top with another English muffin half and close pie iron. Hold pie iron over the fire, turning occasionally, for 5 to 7 minutes. Remove iron from fire and open carefully with a hot pad or oven mitt. Repeat with remaining ingredients.

Equipment needed:
matches
non-stick cooking spray
medium bowl
fork
pie iron
hot pad or oven mitt

Quick tip:
Prepare scrambled eggs at home by whisking together 8 to 10 eggs and 2 tablespoons milk. Cook eggs over medium heat and pack in an airtight container. Place in cooler until ready to prepare recipe.

Taco Tents

Makes 4 servings

2 tubes of 8 refrigerated crescent rolls
1 lb. prepared taco meat
2 C. shredded cheese, any kind

Salsa, tomatoes, lettuce and/or sour cream, optional

Build a flaming campfire. Generously grease both sides of the pie iron with non-stick cooking spray. Unroll crescent rolls and separate into squares, leaving every two crescent rolls together. There should be 8 squares. Place one square on one side of the pie iron. Spoon some of the prepared taco meat and shredded cheese onto square. Top with another crescent roll square. Close iron and hold over flames for 3 minutes on each side, until crescent squares are golden brown. Remove iron from fire and open carefully with a hot pad or oven mitt. If desired, garnish tacos with salsa, tomatoes, lettuce and/ or sour cream. Repeat with remaining ingredients.

Equipment needed:
matches
non-stick cooking spray
spoon
pie iron
hot pad or oven mitt

Quick tip:
Prepare taco meat at home by browning 1 pound ground beef and mixing with ½ cup water and 1 envelope of taco seasoning. Pack in an airtight container and place in cooler until ready to prepare recipe.

Reubens on the Fire

Makes 2 servings

2 slices Swiss cheese
4 slices rye bread
4 to 6 slices corned beef

4 to 6 T. sauerkraut
2 to 4 T. Thousand Island dressing

Build a flaming campfire. Generously grease both sides of the pie iron with non-stick cooking spray. Assemble sandwich by placing one Swiss cheese slice on one slice of rye bread. Top with 2 to 3 slices of corned beef, 2 to 3 tablespoons of sauerkraut, 1 to 2 tablespoons Thousand Island dressing and another slice of rye bread. Place sandwich on one side of the pie iron. Close iron and hold over flames for 3 to 5 minutes on each side. Remove iron from fire and open carefully with a hot pad or oven mitt. Repeat with remaining ingredients.

Equipment needed:
matches
non-stick cooking spray
measuring spoons
pie iron
hot pad or oven mitt

Meat & Cheese Melts

Makes 2 servings

**2 slices American
  or Swiss cheese**
4 slices white or wheat bread

**4 slices deli style ham,
  turkey or roast beef**

Build a flaming campfire. Generously grease both sides of the pie iron with non-stick cooking spray. Assemble sandwich by placing one cheese slice on one slice of bread. Top with 2 slices of ham, turkey or roast beef and another slice of bread. Place sandwich on one side of the pie iron. Close iron and hold over flames for 3 minutes on each side. Remove iron from fire and open carefully with a hot pad or oven mitt. Repeat with remaining ingredients.

Equipment needed:
matches
non-stick cooking spray
pie iron
hot pad or oven mitt

Barbecue Chicken Pies

Makes 2 servings

1 T. butter, softened
4 slices white bread
4 slices Canadian bacon
2 T. barbecue sauce

½ C. shredded Monterey Jack cheese
1 (10 oz.) can chunk chicken, drained

Build a flaming campfire. Generously grease both sides of the pie iron with non-stick cooking spray. Spread butter over one side of each slice of bread. Place one slice of bread, buttered side out, into one side of the pie iron. Layer with 2 slices Canadian bacon, half of the barbecue sauce, half of the shredded Monterey Jack cheese and half of the chunk chicken. Top with another slice of bread, buttered side out. Close iron and hold over flames for 3 minutes on each side. Remove iron from fire and open carefully with a hot pad or oven mitt. Repeat with remaining ingredients.

Equipment needed:
matches
non-stick cooking spray
knife
pie iron
hot pad or oven mitt

Grilled Roast Beef

Makes 5 servings

1 (4 oz.) can chopped green chilies, drained
2 T. mayonnaise
1 T. Dijon mustard
10 slices rye bread

5 slices Swiss cheese
10 slices deli style roast beef
Salsa or Picante sauce, optional

Build a flaming campfire. Generously grease both sides of the pie iron with non-stick cooking spray. In a small bowl, combine chopped green chilies, mayonnaise and Dijon mustard. Spread mixture on one side of each slice of bread. Assemble sandwich by placing one Swiss cheese slice on the spread side of one slice of bread. Top with 2 slices of beef and another slice of bread, spread side down. Place sandwich on one side of the pie iron. Close iron and hold over flames for 3 minutes on each side. Remove iron from fire and open carefully with a hot pad or oven mitt. If desired, serve with salsa or Picante sauce. Repeat with remaining ingredients.

Equipment needed:
matches
non-stick cooking spray
small bowl
spoon
pie iron
hot pad or oven mitt

Quick tip:
Prepare spread at home by combining chopped green chilies, mayonnaise and Dijon mustard. Pack in an airtight container and place in cooler until ready to prepare recipe.

Pizza Pockets

Makes 2 servings

1 T. butter, softened
4 slices white bread
¼ C. pizza sauce
12 to 18 pepperoni slices

1 (4 oz.) can sliced
mushrooms, drained
½ C. shredded mozzarella
cheese

Build a flaming campfire. Generously grease both sides of the pie iron with non-stick cooking spray. Spread butter over one side of each slice of bread. Place one slice of bread, buttered side out, into one side of the pie iron. Layer half of the pizza sauce, pepperoni slices, mushrooms and shredded mozzarella cheese onto bread slice. Cover with another slice of bread, buttered side out. Close iron and hold over flames for 3 minutes on each side. Remove iron from fire and open carefully with a hot pad or oven mitt. Repeat with remaining ingredients.

Equipment needed:
matches
non-stick cooking spray
knife
can opener
pie iron
hot pad or oven mitt

Grilled Tuna Sandwich

Makes 4 servings

1 (12 oz.) can tuna in water, drained
2 T. mayonnaise

Salt and pepper to taste
8 slices white or wheat bread
4 eggs

Build a flaming campfire. Generously grease both sides of the pie iron with non-stick cooking spray. In a small bowl, combine drained tuna and mayonnaise. Season with salt and pepper to taste. Spread tuna on one side of 4 slices of bread. Top each slice with another slice of bread. Crack eggs into the bowl and whisk with a fork. Dip tuna sandwiches in egg mixture. Place one sandwich on one side of the pie iron. Close iron and hold over flames for 3 minutes on each side. Remove iron from fire and open carefully with a hot pad or oven mitt. Repeat with remaining sandwiches.

Equipment needed:
matches
non-stick cooking spray
can opener
small bowl
fork
pie iron
hot pad or oven mitt

Quick tip:
Prepare tuna at home by combining tuna and mayonnaise. Pack in an airtight container and place in cooler until ready to prepare recipe.

Hill Billy Burrito

Makes 4 servings

1 lb. prepared taco meat
½ C. salsa

2 C. shredded Cheddar cheese
4 burrito size tortillas

Build a flaming campfire. Generously grease both sides of the pie iron with non-stick cooking spray. Place 1 tortilla on the pie iron. The tortilla should be large enough to cover both sides of the open pie iron. Spoon some of the prepared taco meat, salsa and shredded cheese onto one side of the tortilla. Fold remaining half of the tortilla over the filling and fold edges in to make a square packet. Close iron and hold over flames for 3 minutes on each side, until tortilla is golden brown. Remove iron from fire and open carefully with a hot pad or oven mitt. Repeat with remaining ingredients.

Equipment needed:
matches
non-stick cooking spray
spoon
pie iron
hot pad or oven mitt

Quick tip:
Prepare taco meat at home by browning 1 pound ground beef and mixing with ½ cup water and 1 envelope of taco seasoning. Pack in an airtight container and place in cooler until ready to prepare recipe.

Grilled Cheese Perfection

Makes 1 serving

1 T. butter, softened
2 slices white bread
**2 slices American or Cheddar
  cheese**

1 slice tomato

Build a flaming campfire. Generously grease both sides of the pie iron with non-stick cooking spray. Spread butter over one side of each slice of bread. Place one slice of bread, buttered side out, into one side of the pie iron. Layer with one cheese slice, tomato slice and remaining cheese slice. Cover with remaining slice of bread, buttered side out. Close iron and hold over flames for 3 minutes on each side. Remove iron from fire and open carefully with a hot pad or oven mitt.

Equipment needed:
matches
non-stick cooking spray
knife
pie iron
hot pad or oven mitt

Apple or Cherry Turnovers

Makes 4 servings

2 T. butter, softened
8 slices white bread

1 (12 oz.) can apple or cherry
pie filling

Build a flaming campfire. Generously grease both sides of the pie iron with non-stick cooking spray. Spread butter over one side of each slice of bread. Place one slice of bread, buttered side out, into one side of the pie iron. Spoon some of the apple or cherry pie filling into the center of the bread slice. Cover with another slice of bread, buttered side out. Close iron and hold over flames for 2 to 3 minutes on each side. Remove iron from fire and open carefully with a hot pad or oven mitt. Repeat with remaining ingredients.

Equipment needed:
matches
non-stick cooking spray
knife
can opener
spoon
pie iron
hot pad or oven mitt

Peanut Butter Chocolate Treats

Makes 2 servings

1 T. butter, softened
4 slices white bread
3 T. creamy or crunchy peanut butter

¼ C. chocolate chips

Build a flaming campfire. Generously grease both sides of the pie iron with non-stick cooking spray. Spread butter over one side of each slice of bread. Place one slice of bread, buttered side out, into one side of the pie iron. Spread half of the peanut butter over the bread slice. Sprinkle half of the chocolate chips over the peanut butter. Cover with another slice of bread, buttered side out. Close iron and hold over flames for 2 to 3 minutes on each side. Remove iron from fire and open carefully with a hot pad or oven mitt. Repeat with remaining ingredients.

Equipment needed:
matches
non-stick cooking spray
knife
pie iron
hot pad or oven mitt

Sweet Peach Pocket

Makes 1 serving

2 slices white bread
1 T. butter, softened
1 peach half, pitted

1 marshmallow
Powdered sugar

Build a flaming campfire. Generously grease both sides of the pie iron with non-stick cooking spray. Spread butter over one side of each slice of bread. Place one slice of bread, buttered side out, into one side of the pie iron. Lay peach half over bread slice and place marshmallow inside the pitted peach. Top with remaining slice of bread, buttered side out. Close iron and hold over flames for 2 to 3 minutes on each side. Remove iron from fire and open carefully with a hot pad or oven mitt. Dust with powdered sugar.

Equipment needed:
matches
non-stick cooking spray
knife
pie iron
hot pad or oven mitt

Banana Rafts

Makes 2 servings

1 T. butter, softened
4 slices white bread
3 T. creamy or crunchy peanut butter

1 banana, peeled
1 to 2 T. brown sugar

Build a flaming campfire. Generously grease both sides of the pie iron with non-stick cooking spray. Spread butter over one side of each slice of bread. Place one slice of bread, buttered side out, into one side of the pie iron. Spread half of the peanut butter over the bread slice. Slice banana in half lengthwise and then cut each side in half. There should be 4 banana pieces. Lay 2 of the banana pieces over peanut butter and sprinkle with half of the brown sugar. Cover with another slice of bread, buttered side out. Close iron and hold over flames for 2 to 3 minutes on each side. Remove iron from fire and open carefully with a hot pad or oven mitt. Repeat with remaining ingredients.

Equipment needed:
matches
non-stick cooking spray
knife
pie iron
hot pad or oven mitt

Wrapped in Foil

Wrapped Apples

Makes 2 servings

2 Granny Smith apples, cored   **½ tsp. cinnamon**
2 T. brown sugar

Build a campfire. Core apples and fill the core of each apple with 1 tablespoon brown sugar and ¼ teaspoon cinnamon. Wrap each apple completely in a large piece of aluminum foil, twisting the extra foil at the top to make a handle. Place wrapped apples directly in the coals of the campfire and cook for 5 to 10 minutes, until softened. Using long tongs, remove apples from fire. Using a hot pad or oven mitt, slowly unwrap apples, being careful not to spill any hot sugar. Eat apples with a fork.

Equipment needed:
matches
apple corer or sharp knife
aluminum foil
measuring spoons
long tongs
hot pad or oven mitt
2 forks

Campfire Vidalias

Makes 4 servings

4 Vidalia onions
4 T. butter or margarine

4 cloves garlic, minced
Salt to taste

Build a campfire. Peel the outer skin from each onion and cut each onion into quarters, keeping each onion together. Place 1 tablespoon butter and ¼ of the minced garlic in the center of each onion. Wrap each onion in a double layer of aluminum foil. Place wrapped onions directly in the coals of the campfire and cook for 30 to 40 minutes. Using long tongs, remove onions from fire. Using a hot pad or oven mitt, slowly unwrap onions and season with salt to taste.

Equipment needed:
matches
sharp knife
aluminum foil
long tongs
hot pad or oven mitt

Tomato & Mushroom Pouch

Makes 2 to 4 servings

3 to 4 large tomatoes, cut into wedges
1 (8 oz.) pkg. whole mushrooms, cleaned and cut in half

1 large onion, cut into wedges
½ (16 oz.) bottle French or Italian salad dressing
Salt and pepper to taste

Build a campfire. Place tomato wedges, mushrooms and onion wedges on a large piece of aluminum foil. Pour salad dressing over vegetables and season with salt and pepper to taste. Wrap aluminum up and over vegetables to seal the packet. Wrap packet again in aluminum foil. Place wrapped packet directly in the coals of the campfire and cook for 20 to 25 minutes. Using long tongs, remove packet from fire. Using a hot pad or oven mitt, slowly unwrap packet.

Equipment needed:
matches
aluminum foil
long tongs
hot pad or oven mitt

Chili Cheese Fries

Makes 4 servings

**1 (26 oz.) bag frozen
French fries**

**1 (15 oz.) can chili with beans
1 (15 oz.) jar Cheez Whiz**

Build a campfire. Place frozen French fries, chili with beans and Cheez Whiz on a large piece of aluminum foil. You may have to divide ingredients into two packets. Mix ingredients together slightly and wrap aluminum up and over fries to seal the packet. Wrap packet(s) again in aluminum foil. Place wrapped packet(s) directly in the coals of the campfire and cook for 20 to 25 minutes, until fries are softened and cooked. Using long tongs, remove packet from fire. Using a hot pad or oven mitt, slowly unwrap packet.

Equipment needed:
matches
aluminum foil
can opener
long tongs
hot pad or oven mitt

Cinnamon Roll Cups

Makes 4 serving

4 oranges
1 tube of 10 refrigerated
    biscuits

4 tsp. cinnamon
½ C. powdered sugar
4 tsp. milk

Build a campfire. Cut top ⅓ from each orange and scrape out pulp. Eat or discard pulp. Separate tube into individual biscuits. Mash biscuits into round circles. Sprinkle 4 of the biscuits with 1 teaspoon cinnamon and ½ tablespoon powdered sugar. Top biscuits with another biscuit and sprinkle with 1 teaspoon cinnamon and ½ tablespoon powdered sugar. Divide remaining 2 biscuits into 4 parts. Flatten four remaining parts and place on top of each biscuit. Roll up layered biscuits and place inside the hollowed orange peel cups. Divide remaining 4 tablespoons powdered sugar into each orange and pour 1 teaspoon milk into each orange. Replace top peel of orange and wrap each orange in aluminum foil. Place wrapped oranges directly in the coals of the campfire and cook for 30 minutes. Using long tongs, remove oranges from fire. Using a hot pad or oven mitt, slowly unwrap oranges and peel oranges to reveal cooked biscuits.

Equipment needed:
matches
sharp knife
spoon
measuring spoons
aluminum foil
long tongs
hot pad or oven mitt

Blueberry Muffin Spheres

Makes 6 servings

6 oranges
2 (7 or 8 oz.) boxes blueberry
  muffin mix

Build a campfire. Cut top ⅓ from each orange and scrape out pulp. Eat or discard pulp. In a medium bowl, prepare muffin mix according to box instructions (be sure to pack the extra eggs, oil or milk needed). Spoon muffin mix evenly into hollowed oranges. Replace top peel of orange and wrap each orange in aluminum foil. Place wrapped oranges directly in the coals of the campfire, making sure the oranges sit upright, so as not to spill the batter. Bake for 5 to 10 minutes, until muffins are done. Using long tongs, remove oranges from fire. Using a hot pad or oven mitt, slowly unwrap oranges and peel oranges to reveal cooked muffins.

Equipment needed:
matches
sharp knife
spoon
medium bowl
aluminum foil
long tongs
hot pad or oven mitt

Onion Carousel

Makes 1 serving

1 large Vidalia, Walla-Walla
or Mayan Sweet onion
Garlic powder

Pepper
1 slice bacon
1 T. butter or margarine

Build a campfire. Peel the outer skin from each onion and cut and "X" from the top of the onion to within 1" from the bottom. Cut another "X" from the top of the onion to make 8 sections, keeping sections attached at the bottom. Sprinkle onion with garlic powder and pepper to taste. Cut bacon slice in half lengthwise. Weave bacon pieces in a criss-cross pattern between wedges. Place butter on top of onion and wrap onion in a double layer of aluminum foil. Place wrapped onion directly in the coals of the campfire and cook for 45 minutes, turning every 15 minutes. Using long tongs, remove onion from fire. Using a hot pad or oven mitt, slowly unwrap onion.

Equipment needed:
matches
sharp knife
aluminum foil
long tongs
hot pad or oven mitt

Silver Garlic Chicken

Makes 2 servings

1 large skinless boneless chicken breast	**1 medium green bell pepper, sliced**
½ tsp. minced garlic	**Pinch of oregano**
1 small onion, sliced	**Pinch of curry powder**

Build a campfire. Place chicken breast, minced garlic, sliced onions and sliced green bell peppers on a large piece of aluminum foil. Sprinkle with oregano and curry powder. Wrap aluminum up and over ingredients to seal the packet. Wrap packet again in aluminum foil. Place wrapped packet directly in the coals of the campfire and cook for about 20 minutes, turning after every 5 minutes. Using long tongs, remove packet from fire. Using a hot pad or oven mitt, slowly unwrap packet.

Equipment needed:
matches
sharp knife
aluminum foil
long tongs
hot pad or oven mitt

Oriental Chicken

Makes 1 serving

1 skinless boneless chicken breast
1 C. frozen mixed vegetables
2 tsp. soy sauce

Pinch of garlic salt
Pinch of cayenne pepper, optional
1 T. brown sugar

Build a campfire. Place chicken breast and frozen mixed vegetables on a large piece of aluminum foil. Sprinkle with soy sauce, garlic salt, cayenne pepper and brown sugar. Wrap aluminum up and over ingredients to seal the packet. Wrap packet again in aluminum foil. Place wrapped packet directly in the coals of the campfire and cook for about 20 to 30 minutes, until chicken is cooked throughout. Using long tongs, remove packet from fire. Using a hot pad or oven mitt, slowly unwrap packet.

Equipment needed:
matches
aluminum foil
long tongs
hot pad or oven mitt

Hobo Burgers

Makes 1 serving

1 hamburger patty
2 carrots, peeled and sliced
1 medium potato, cubed
1 small sweet onion, diced

Salt and pepper to taste
Garlic salt
2 T. butter

Build a campfire. Place hamburger patty, sliced carrots, cubed potatoes and diced sweet onions on a large piece of aluminum foil. Season with salt, pepper and garlic salt to taste. Place butter on top of ingredients. Wrap aluminum up and over ingredients to seal the packet. Wrap packet again in aluminum foil. Place wrapped packet directly in the coals of the campfire and cook for 45 minutes, until burger is cooked throughout. Using long tongs, remove packet from fire. Using a hot pad or oven mitt, slowly unwrap packet.

Equipment needed:
matches
aluminum foil
sharp knife
long tongs
hot pad or oven mitt

Spam Packs

Makes 2 servings

1 (12 oz.) can Spam, cut ¼" thick
1 (20 oz.) can crushed pineapple, drained
1 (15 oz.) can yams, drained
1 (15 oz.) can whole white potatoes, drained
2 T. butter
1 C. dark brown sugar

Build a campfire. Set out two large pieces of aluminum foil. Divide Spam slices, drained pineapple, drained yams and drained white potatoes onto aluminum foil pieces. Place 1 tablespoon butter on top of ingredients in each packet. Sprinkle brown sugar evenly over ingredients in packets. Wrap aluminum up and over ingredients to seal the packets. Wrap packets again in aluminum foil. Place wrapped packets directly in the coals of the campfire and cook for 20 minutes, turning once. Using long tongs, remove packets from fire. Using a hot pad or oven mitt, slowly unwrap packets.

Equipment needed:
matches
sharp knife
can opener
aluminum foil
long tongs
hot pad or oven mitt

Lemon Chicken

Makes 2 servings

1 lemon, sliced thin
2 skinless boneless chicken
breast halves

1 clove garlic, crushed
Italian seasoning to taste
1 T. butter or margarine

Build a campfire. Place 4 lemon slices on a large piece of aluminum foil. Lay chicken breast halves over lemons. Lay 2 lemon slices over chicken and sprinkle with crushed garlic and Italian seasoning to taste. Top with butter. Wrap aluminum up and over ingredients to seal the packet. Wrap packet again in aluminum foil. Place wrapped packet directly in the coals of the campfire and cook for 40 minutes, turning after every 10 minutes. Using long tongs, remove packet from fire. Using a hot pad or oven mitt, slowly unwrap packet.

Equipment needed:
matches
sharp knife
aluminum foil
long tongs
hot pad or oven mitt

Hot Baked Fish

Makes 2 servings

2 trout, salmon, flounder or red snapper filets
1 T. olive oil
2 T. white wine, optional

Juice of ½ lemon
Salt and pepper to taste
Fresh chopped dill

Build a campfire. Place fish filets onto a large piece of aluminum foil. Sprinkle olive oil, white wine and lemon juice over fish. Season with salt, pepper and fresh chopped dill to taste. Wrap aluminum up and over ingredients to seal the packet. Wrap packet again in aluminum foil. Place wrapped packet directly in the coals of the campfire and cook for about 30 minutes. Using long tongs, remove packet from fire. Using a hot pad or oven mitt, slowly unwrap packet.

Equipment needed:
matches
sharp knife
aluminum foil
long tongs
hot pad or oven mitt

Foil Wrapped Apricot Chicken

Makes 4 servings

4 skinless boneless chicken breasts
1 to 2 tsp. paprika

Salt and pepper to taste
4 T. apricot preserves
2 T. Dijon mustard

Build a campfire. Set out four large pieces of aluminum foil. Divide chicken breasts onto aluminum foil pieces. Sprinkle paprika, salt and pepper evenly over chicken breasts. Spoon apricot preserves and Dijon mustard evenly onto each chicken breast. Wrap aluminum up and over ingredients to seal the packets. Wrap packets again in aluminum foil. Place wrapped packets directly in the coals of the campfire and cook for 20 to 30 minutes, until chicken is cooked throughout. Using long tongs, remove packets from fire. Using a hot pad or oven mitt, slowly unwrap packets.

Equipment needed:
matches
spoon
aluminum foil
long tongs
hot pad or oven mitt

Shrimp Packets

1 lb. shrimp, peeled and
    deveined
¼ C. butter or margarine,
    cut into pieces

1 clove garlic, minced
½ tsp. pepper
1 tsp. salt
1 C. parsley flakes

    Build a campfire. Lay shrimp on a large piece of aluminum foil.
Top with butter pieces, minced garlic, pepper, salt and parsley flakes.
Wrap aluminum up and over ingredients to seal the packet. Wrap
packet again in aluminum foil. Place wrapped packet directly in the
coals of the campfire and cook for 10 to 15 minutes, until shrimp is
fully cooked. Using long tongs, remove packets from fire. Using a hot
pad or oven mitt, slowly unwrap packets.

Equipment needed:
matches
aluminum foil
long tongs
hot pad or oven mitt

Hawaiian Ham Delight

Makes 1 serving

2 pieces thick sliced ham
1 potato, peeled and cubed
2 carrots, peeled and sliced

1 (20 oz.) can crushed
** pineapple**
1 tsp. brown sugar

   Build a campfire. Place ham slices, cubed potatoes, sliced carrots, pineapple pieces and brown sugar on a large piece of aluminum foil. Sprinkle with some of the pineapple juice from can. Wrap aluminum up and over ingredients to seal the packet. Wrap packet again in aluminum foil. Place wrapped packet directly in the coals of the campfire and cook for about 20 minutes, turning after every 5 minutes. Using long tongs, remove packet from fire. Using a hot pad or oven mitt, slowly unwrap packet.

Equipment needed:
matches
vegetable peeler
sharp knife
can opener
aluminum foil
long tongs
hot pad or oven mitt

Pork Chop Package

Makes 1 serving

1 pork chop
1 large potato, cubed
1 large carrot, peeled and sliced

1 onion, cut into wedges
Lawry's seasoning salt

Build a campfire. Place pork chop, cubed potatoes, sliced carrots and onion wedges on a large piece of aluminum foil. Sprinkle with seasoning salt to taste. Wrap aluminum up and over ingredients to seal the packet. Wrap packet again in aluminum foil. Place wrapped packet directly in the coals of the campfire and cook for 30 minutes, turning after 15 minutes. Using long tongs, remove packet from fire. Using a hot pad or oven mitt, slowly unwrap packet.

Equipment needed:
matches
sharp knife
vegetable peeler
aluminum foil
long tongs
hot pad or oven mitt

Three Minute Pizza

Makes 10 servings

1 pkg. 5 Pita bread slices
1 (15 oz.) can pizza sauce
4 C. shredded mozzarella
  cheese

Pepperoni slices
Additional pizza toppings,
  optional

    Build a campfire. Cut each pita bread in half to make 10 pita pockets. Spoon pizza sauce into pita pockets, spreading evenly. Add shredded mozzarella cheese, pepperoni slices and any additional toppings desired. Wrap each pita pocket in aluminum foil. Place wrapped packets directly in the coals of the campfire and cook for 3 minutes, turning once. Using long tongs, remove packets from fire. Using a hot pad or oven mitt, slowly unwrap packets.

Equipment needed:
matches
sharp knife
can opener
aluminum foil
long tongs
hot pad or oven mitt

Honey Mustard Chicken Packets

Makes 4 servings

4 skinless boneless chicken breasts

4 potatoes, quartered lengthwise

1 green or red bell pepper, cut into strips

8 to 12 T. honey mustard barbecue sauce

Build a campfire. Set out four large pieces of aluminum foil. Divide chicken breasts, potatoes, and bell pepper strips onto aluminum foil pieces. Drizzle 2 to 3 tablespoons honey mustard barbecue sauce over each packet. Wrap aluminum up and over ingredients to seal the packets. Wrap packets again in aluminum foil. Place wrapped packets directly in the coals of the campfire and cook for 20 to 30 minutes, until chicken is cooked throughout. Using long tongs, remove packets from fire. Using a hot pad or oven mitt, slowly unwrap packets.

Equipment needed:
matches
sharp knife
aluminum foil
long tongs
hot pad or oven mitt

Easy Ranch Chicken

Makes 6 servings

1 (.4 oz.) env. Ranch dressing mix	**6 skinless boneless chicken breast halves**
¾ C. corn flakes, crushed	**¼ C. butter, melted**
¾ C. grated Parmesan cheese	**1 red bell pepper, cut into strips**

Build a campfire. Set out six large pieces of aluminum foil. In a medium bowl combine Ranch dressing mix, crushed corn flakes and Parmesan cheese. Dip chicken breast halves into melted butter and roll in crushed corn flakes mixture. Set one chicken breast half on each piece of aluminum foil and top with some of the red bell pepper strips. Wrap aluminum up and over ingredients to seal the packets. Wrap packets again in aluminum foil. Place wrapped packets directly in the coals of the campfire and cook for 20 to 30 minutes, until chicken is cooked throughout. Using long tongs, remove packets from fire. Using a hot pad or oven mitt, slowly unwrap packets.

Equipment needed:
matches
medium bowl
spoon
aluminum foil
long tongs
hot pad or oven mitt

Banana Boats

Makes 6 servings

6 large bananas
2 C. chocolate chips

1 (10½ oz.) pkg. miniature marshmallows

Build a campfire. Set out six large pieces of aluminum foil. Leaving the peels on the bananas, remove the stems. Make a cut in each banana from top to bottom lengthwise. Spoon out a little of the banana flesh. Stuff with chocolate chips and marshmallows. Wrap each banana in aluminum foil. Place wrapped bananas directly in the coals of the campfire and cook for about 5 minutes, until chocolate is melted. Using long tongs, remove bananas from fire. Using a hot pad or oven mitt, slowly unwrap bananas. Eat banana boats with a spoon right from the peel.

Equipment needed:
matches
sharp knife
aluminum foil
long tongs
hot pad or oven mitt
6 spoons

Pineapple Upside Down Cake

Makes 2 servings

1 cake donut	**1 T. butter**
2 pineapple rings	**4 tsp. brown sugar**

Build a campfire. Set out two large pieces of aluminum foil. Cut cake donut in half and set one half on each piece of foil. Lay one pineapple slice on each donut half and dot pineapple slices with butter. Sprinkle brown sugar over each slice. Wrap aluminum foil up around ingredients and seal tightly. Place wrapped cakes directly in the coals of the campfire and cook for about 10 to 15 minutes. Using long tongs, remove packets from fire. Using a hot pad or oven mitt, slowly unwrap packets.

Equipment needed:
matches
sharp knife
aluminum foil
long tongs
hot pad or oven mitt

Pears in Caramel Sauce

Makes 2 servings

2 T. sweetened butter　　**1 Comice or Anjou pear**
2 T. brown sugar　　　　　**1 orange, halved**
Pinch of cinnamon

Build a campfire. Set out two large pieces of aluminum foil. Cut pear in half and remove core and stem. In a small bowl, combine butter, brown sugar and cinnamon. Lay each pear half on a piece of the aluminum foil. Scoop half of the butter mixture into the cored side of each pear. Squeeze orange juice over each pear. Wrap aluminum foil up around pears and seal tightly. Place wrapped pears directly in the coals of the campfire and cook for about 20 to 30 minutes, until completely softened. Using long tongs, remove packets from fire. Using a hot pad or oven mitt, slowly unwrap packets, being careful not to spill hot caramel sauce.

Equipment needed:
matches
sharp knife
small bowl
spoon
aluminum foil
long tongs
hot pad or oven mitt

In a Skillet

Fireside Fondue

Makes 6 to 8 servings

2 C. shredded Swiss cheese
2 T. flour
¼ tsp. paprika

1 (10¾ oz.) can cream of
 mushroom or broccoli soup
½ C. beer or white wine

    Preheat camping stove or place grilling grate over campfire. Place shredded Swiss cheese, flour, paprika, cream of mushroom soup and beer in a cast iron skillet and place skillet over heat. Cook fondue, stirring frequently, until cheese is melted and mixture is heated throughout. Serve fondue with fresh veggies, crusty bread or crackers.

Equipment needed:
matches
cast iron skillet
measuring spoons
can opener
cooking spoon

Quick tip:
Prepare dry mixture at home by combining shredded Swiss cheese, flour and paprika. Pack in a ziplock bag and place in cooler until ready to prepare recipe.

Campfire Green Beans

Makes 6 servings

2 T. olive oil
1 Vidalia onion, chopped
1 clove garlic, minced
¼ C. slivered almonds

3 (14½ oz.) cans French cut
green beans, drained
Salt and pepper to taste

Preheat camping stove or place grilling grate over campfire. Place olive oil, chopped onions, minced garlic and slivered almonds in a cast iron skillet and place skillet over heat. Sauté mixture until onions are tender, about 5 minutes. Add drained green beans to skillet and season with salt and pepper to taste. Cook until green beans are heated throughout.

Equipment needed:
matches
cast iron skillet
measuring spoons
can opener
cooking spoon

Quick tip:
Prepare entire recipe at home and pack green beans mixture in a ziplock bag and place in cooler. At campsite, place mixture in a cast iron skillet over stove or fire until heated throughout.

Baked Beans & Sausage

1 (8 oz.) pkg. smoked sausage
  links, sliced ½" thick
1½ C. chopped onions
¾ C. barbecue sauce
2 T. syrup
2 T. apple cider vinegar

1 (16 oz.) can red kidney
  beans, rinsed
1 (16 oz.) can pinto beans,
  rinsed
1 (16 oz.) can black beans,
  rinsed

Preheat camping stove or place grilling grate over campfire. Place sausage slices in a cast iron skillet and place skillet over heat. Cook sausage for 3 minutes on each side or until evenly browned. Remove sausage slices to a plate. Add chopped onions to skillet and cook until softened. Add barbecue sauce, syrup, apple cider vinegar and a little water. Bring mixture to a boil. Open all cans and add rinsed kidney beans, pinto beans and black beans to skillet. Return sausage slices to skillet. Mix well and cover skillet with lid. Heat, stirring occasionally, for about 15 minutes.

Equipment needed:
matches
cast iron skillet
sharp knife
plate
measuring spoons
can opener
cooking spoon

Ranch Style Veggies

Makes 4 servings

1 T. vegetable oil
1 (.4 oz.) env. Ranch dressing mix
2 medium carrots, peeled and thinly sliced

2 medium yellow squash, thinly sliced
2 medium zucchini, thinly sliced

Preheat camping stove or place grilling grate over campfire. Place vegetable oil and Ranch dressing mix in a cast iron skillet and place skillet over heat. Mix well and add sliced carrots. Cook carrots for 4 to 5 minutes, until tender but crisp. Add squash and zucchini and cook for an additional 4 to 5 minutes, until vegetables are tender. Remove vegetables from skillet with a slotted spoon.

Equipment needed:
matches
cast iron skillet
vegetable peeler
sharp knife
slotted spoon

Egg Crackle

Makes 6 servings

1 lb. bacon, chopped
12 eggs
¼ C. milk

Salt and pepper to taste
1 individual size bag cheese
   crackers

    Preheat camping stove or place grilling grate over campfire. Place chopped bacon in a cast iron skillet and place skillet over heat. Cook bacon to desired crispness and drain grease from skillet. In a medium bowl, combine eggs and milk. Add salt and pepper to taste. Add egg mixture to skillet and mix with bacon pieces. Cook until eggs are set. Crush cheese crackers into small pieces and sprinkle over eggs.

Equipment needed:
matches
cast iron skillet
medium bowl
spoon or fork

Early Bird Nests

Makes 2 servings

1 T. vegetable oil
2 slices white or wheat bread
2 eggs

Bacon bits
Salt and pepper to taste

Preheat camping stove or place grilling grate over campfire. Place vegetable oil in a cast iron skillet and place skillet over heat. Tear out the center of each slice of bread and set in skillet. Toast bread centers until lightly browned, turning once. Remove from skillet and set aside. Set bread crusts (with a hole in the center) in skillet and toast until lightly browned on one side. Turn crusts over and crack one egg in the center of each hole. Cook until eggs are set. Top with bacon bits. Season with salt and pepper to taste. Serve with toasted bread centers on the side.

Equipment needed:
matches
cast iron skillet
measuring spoons

Kayak Tuna Mac

Makes 2 servings

2 pkgs. Kraft Easy Mac
1 (6 oz.) can tuna in water,
  drained

1 (8½ oz.) can green peas,
  drained

Preheat camping stove or place grilling grate over campfire. Place 1 ¼ cups water in a cast iron skillet and place skillet over heat. Bring water to a boil and add noodles from Easy Mac packets. Boil noodles for 3 minutes. Remove skillet from heat and pour out excess water, leaving a little water in the skillet. Add cheese sauce packets, drained tuna and drained peas. Mix well. Return skillet to heat until mixture is heated throughout.

Equipment needed:
matches
cast iron skillet
can opener
cooking spoon

Wild & Sloppy Joes

Makes 8 servings

2 lbs. ground beef
1 C. chopped celery
½ C. chopped onions
1 (10¾ oz.) can tomato soup
¼ C. ketchup
1 T. white vinegar

¼ C. brown sugar
1½ tsp. Worcestershire sauce
½ tsp. salt
¼ tsp. garlic powder
8 hamburger buns

Preheat camping stove or place grilling grate over campfire. Place ground beef in a cast iron skillet and place skillet over heat. Cook ground beef until evenly browned. Add chopped celery and chopped onions. Cook until celery and onions are tender and drain grease from skillet. Add tomato soup, ketchup, white vinegar, brown sugar and Worcestershire sauce. Mix well and season with salt and garlic powder. Let mixture simmer, stirring frequently, until heated throughout. Spoon mixture onto hamburger buns.

Equipment needed:
matches
cast iron skillet
sharp knife
can opener
measuring spoons
cooking spoon

Quick tip:
Chop onions and celery at home and pack in an airtight container. Place in cooler until ready to prepare recipe. Can also pack brown sugar, salt and garlic powder in a ziplock bag.

Beer Battered Fish

Makes 8 servings

½ C. vegetable oil
1 C. beer

2 lbs. trout filets
1 C. Bisquick baking mix

Preheat camping stove or place grilling grate over campfire. Place vegetable oil in a cast iron skillet and place skillet over heat. In a medium bowl, combine Bisquick baking mix and beer. Mix well. Dip fish filets in batter. Using a pair of tongs, remove fish from batter and shake off excess. Place battered fish in hot oil in skillet. Fry fish until golden brown, about 3 to 4 minutes on each side.

Equipment needed:
matches
cast iron skillet
medium bowl
spoon
measuring cups
pair of tongs

Cowboy Casserole

Makes 5 servings

½ lb. bacon
1 lb. ground beef
1 small onion, chopped
2 (15 oz.) cans pork n' beans

⅓ C. barbecue sauce
1 tube of 10 refrigerated biscuits

Preheat camping stove or place grilling grate over campfire. Place bacon in a cast iron skillet and place skillet over heat. Cook bacon to desired crispness and remove from skillet to paper towels. When bacon has drained, crumble and set aside. Add ground beef and chopped onions to skillet and cook until ground beef is evenly browned and onions are tender. Drain grease from skillet and add crumbled bacon, pork n' beans and barbecue sauce. Bring mixture to a low boil. Separate tube into individual biscuits and place biscuits over ingredients in skillet. Cover skillet and let simmer for about 10 minutes, or until biscuits are golden brown. Place two biscuits on each plate and spoon casserole over biscuits.

Equipment needed:
matches
cast iron skillet
paper towels
sharp knife
can opener
cooking spoon

Walking Tacos

Makes 4 serving

1 lb. prepared taco meat	**Chopped tomatoes**
Shredded lettuce	**Sour cream**
½ C. shredded Cheddar cheese	**4 individual size bags Doritos**

Preheat camping stove or place grilling grate over campfire. Place prepared taco meat in a cast iron skillet and place skillet over heat. Cook until taco meat is heated throughout. Open bags of Doritos and lightly crush the chips. Spoon heated taco meat into bags and top with shredded Cheddar cheese, shredded lettuce, chopped tomatoes and sour cream. Eat walking tacos with a fork right from the bag.

Equipment needed:
matches
cast iron skillet
spoon
4 forks

Quick tip:
Prepare taco meat at home by browning 1 pound ground beef and mixing with ½ cup water and 1 envelope of taco seasoning. Pack in an airtight container and place in cooler until ready to prepare recipe.

Chicken Fajitas

Makes 6 servings

**3 boneless skinless chicken
breast halves**
1 clove garlic, halved
**1 medium green or red bell
pepper, cut into strips**

½ red onion, cut into strips
**1½ C. shredded Cheddar
cheese**
6 flour tortillas
Salsa

Preheat camping stove or place grilling grate over campfire. Rub both sides of each chicken breast with garlic halves. Place chicken breasts in a cast iron skillet and place skillet over heat. Cook until chicken is heated throughout. Remove chicken to a plate and cut into strips. Add green or red pepper strips and onions to skillet and cook until softened. Return chicken to skillet. Spoon ¼ cup shredded Cheddar cheese and some salsa into the center of each tortilla. Fill each tortilla with some of the chicken, peppers and onions mixture. Fold tortillas to enclose mixture.

Equipment needed:
matches
cast iron skillet
plate
sharp knife
cooking spoon

63

Creole Campout

Makes 4 serving

2 T. butter or margarine
1 medium onion, chopped
½ green bell pepper, chopped
½ C. chopped celery
2 T. flour

2 tsp. Cajun seasoning
1 (12 oz.) can tuna in water, drained
1 (15¼ oz.) can whole kernel corn

Preheat camping stove or place grilling grate over campfire. Place butter in a cast iron skillet and place skillet over heat. Cook until butter is melted and add chopped onions, chopped green bell pepper and chopped celery. Cook until vegetables are tender and add flour. Mix well and add Cajun seasoning, drained tuna and corn. Heat for 3 to 5 minutes, stirring occasionally.

Equipment needed:
matches
cast iron skillet
cooking spoon
can opener
measuring spoons

Beans & Texas Toast

Makes 4 servings

1 lb. ground beef　　　　　　**Butter**
1 (15 oz.) can pork n' beans　**Garlic salt**
4 slices Texas Toast

　　Preheat camping stove or place grilling grate over campfire. Place ground beef in a cast iron skillet and place skillet over heat. Cook until ground beef is completely browned and cooked throughout. Add pork n' beans and mix well. Cook until mixture is heated throughout. Meanwhile, spread butter over both sides of each slice of bread and toast over camping stove or campfire. When toast is lightly browned, remove from heat and sprinkle with garlic salt. Spoon ground beef mixture into bowls and eat with toast on the side.

Equipment needed:
matches
cast iron skillet
cooking spoon
can opener
knife
4 bowls
4 forks

Hungry Man's Polish Sausage Dinner

Makes 2 to 4 servings

2 T. vegetable oil
1 pkg. polish sausage
2 potatoes, peeled and
**   chopped**
2 sweet potatoes, peeled
**   and chopped**

1 large onion, chopped
1 green bell pepper, diced
1 red bell pepper, diced
1 yellow squash, chopped

Preheat camping stove or place grilling grate over campfire. Place vegetable oil in an extra large cast iron skillet and place skillet over heat. Add polish sausage, chopped potatoes, chopped sweet potatoes, chopped onions, diced green and red bell peppers and chopped yellow squash. Cook sausage and vegetables until heated throughout. Remove sausages to a plate and cut into pieces. Return sausages to skillet and cook for an additional minute.

Equipment needed:
matches
extra large cast iron skillet
vegetable peeler
sharp knife
plate
cooking spoon

Quick tip:
Prepare polish sausage at home and chop into pieces. Pack in an airtight container and place in cooler until ready to prepare recipe.

Quick & Easy Tomato Casserole

Makes 4 to 6 servings

1 T. vegetable oil
1 lb. ground beef
1 small onion, chopped
1 (14½ oz.) can stewed
   tomatoes in juice

1 (15 oz.) can whole kernel
   corn, drained

Preheat camping stove or place grilling grate over campfire. Place vegetable oil in a cast iron skillet and place skillet over heat. Add ground beef and cook until evenly browned. Add chopped onions and cook until onions are tender. Add stewed tomatoes in juice and drained corn. Cook until mixture is heated throughout. Spoon into bowls.

Equipment needed:
matches
cast iron skillet
can opener
cooking spoon
4 to 6 bowls

Pork Chop Dinner

Makes 2 servings

2 pork chops
2 potatoes, peeled and chopped
1 onion, chopped

1 small head cabbage, shredded
1 (10¾ oz.) can cream of mushroom soup

Preheat camping stove or place grilling grate over campfire. Place pork chops in a cast iron skillet and place skillet over heat. Cook pork chops until browned on both sides, turning once. Add chopped potatoes and chopped onions to skillet and sautéed until browned. Add shredded cabbage and cream of mushroom soup. Fill empty soup can with water and add to skillet. Mix slightly. Add lid to skillet and cook over heat for about 20 minutes, until potatoes are tender and mixture is heated throughout.

Equipment needed:
matches
cast iron skillet
vegetable peeler
sharp knife
can opener
cooking spoon

In a Dutch Oven

Fiesta Chicken Soup

Makes 10 to 12 servings

1 (32 oz.) can chicken broth

2 (14½ oz.) cans whole kernel corn, undrained

1 (14 to 16 oz.) can Ranch style beans

1 (10 oz.) can diced tomatoes with green chilies

2 chicken bouillon cubes

1 (10 oz.) can white chunk chicken, drained

1 (8 oz.) box Velveeta light cheese

Build a campfire using briquettes and set up tripod for a Dutch oven. Open all cans and place chicken broth, corn in juice, Ranch style beans, diced tomatoes with green chilies, chicken bouillon cubes and drained white chunk chicken in Dutch oven. Hang Dutch oven over heat. Cook mixture, stirring occasionally, until heated throughout. Cut Velveeta cheese into cubes. Add cheese cubes to soup and stir until cheese is melted.

Equipment needed:
matches
briquettes
Dutch oven
can opener
cooking spoon
knife
ladle

Big Pond Soup

Makes 24 servings

1 lb. lean ground beef
1 (15 oz.) can carrots, drained
1 (15¼ oz.) can whole kernel corn
1 (15 oz.) can green beans
1 (15 oz.) can peas
1 (15 oz.) can sliced potatoes
1 (15 oz.) can mixed vegetables

1 (10 oz.) can asparagus
1 (46 oz.) can tomato juice
1 medium head cabbage, chopped
½ tsp. garlic powder
1 tsp. onion powder
Salt and pepper to taste

Build a campfire using briquettes and set up tripod for a Dutch oven. Place ground beef in Dutch oven and hang Dutch oven over heat. Cook ground beef until evenly browned. Drain pot and crumble the ground beef, leaving ground beef in the pot. Open all of the cans and drain liquid only from the carrots. Add drained carrots, corn in juice, green beans in juice, peas in juice, sliced potatoes in juice, mixed vegetables in juice, asparagus in juice, tomato juice and chopped cabbage to the Dutch oven. Season with garlic powder and onion powder. Cook soup until heated throughout and cabbage is tender. Add salt and pepper to taste.

Equipment needed:
matches
briquettes
sharp knife
Dutch oven
cooking spoon
can opener
measuring spoons
ladle

Hobo Stew

Makes 4 servings

1 lb. ground beef   **1 (28 oz.) can baked beans**
1 large onion, chopped   **1 large can water**

Build a campfire using briquettes and set up tripod for a Dutch oven. Place ground beef in Dutch oven and hang Dutch oven over heat. Cook ground beef for about 5 minutes, until evenly browned. Drain pot of grease and add chopped onions and baked beans. Fill empty baked beans can with water and add to pot. Cook until stew is heated throughout.

Equipment needed:
matches
briquettes
Dutch oven
sharp knife
can opener
ladle

Starry Night Chili

Makes 12 servings

3 lbs. ground beef
3 onions, chopped
10 cloves garlic, minced
3 (15 oz.) cans pork n' beans
3 (15 oz.) cans kidney beans, drained

1 (14½ oz.) can stewed tomatoes
3 T. chili powder
1 (12 oz.) can beer
Salt and pepper to taste

Build a campfire using briquettes and set up tripod for a Dutch oven. Place ground beef in Dutch oven and hang Dutch oven over heat. Cook ground beef for about 5 minutes, until evenly browned. Add chopped onions and minced garlic and sauté for an additional 5 to 10 minutes. Add pork n' beans, drained kidney beans, stewed tomatoes in juice, chili powder and beer. Reduce heat to low or move pot to outer edge of grate. Cover pot and let simmer for 60 minutes, stirring occasionally. Season with salt and pepper to taste.

Equipment needed:
matches
briquettes
sharp knife
Dutch oven
cooking spoon
can opener
measuring spoons
ladle

Campout Cornbread

Makes 10 to 12 servings

1 C. butter, melted
4 eggs, beaten
3 C. milk
2 C. sugar

2 C. cornmeal
3 C. flour
4 tsp. baking powder
1 tsp. salt

Build a campfire using briquettes and dig a hole in the coals for the Dutch oven. In a large bowl, combine melted butter, eggs and milk. Add sugar, cornmeal, flour, baking powder and salt. Lightly grease a 12" Dutch oven and spoon cornbread mixture into pot. Set Dutch oven in hole. Place lid on Dutch oven and set 14 to 16 briquettes on lid. Bake for 45 minutes or until cornbread is golden brown.

Equipment needed:
matches
briquettes
12" Dutch oven
large bowl
cooking spoon
measuring cups

Quick tip:
Prepare dry mix at home by combining sugar, cornmeal, flour, baking powder and salt. Pack in an airtight container until ready to prepare recipe.

5 Can Soup

Makes 6 servings

1 (14½ oz.) can diced tomatoes
1 (8½ oz.) can mixed vegetables
1 (15 oz.) can white corn, drained

1 (15 oz.) can black beans, rinsed and drained
1 (10½ oz.) can Progresso minestrone soup

Build a campfire using briquettes and set up tripod for a Dutch oven. Open all cans and place diced tomatoes in juice, mixed vegetables in juice, drained corn, drained black beans and minestrone soup in Dutch oven. Hang Dutch oven over heat. Let soup heat for about 20 minutes, stirring occasionally.

Equipment needed:
matches
briquettes
Dutch oven
can opener
cooking spoon
ladle

Breakfast Pizza

Makes 6 to 8 servings

1 lb. sausage
1 (8 oz.) pkg. refrigerated crescent rolls
3 T. diced red bell peppers
3 T. diced green bell peppers
1 C. frozen hash browns, thawed

1 green onion, sliced
1 C. shredded Cheddar cheese
3 eggs, beaten
3 T. milk
½ tsp. salt
1 tsp. pepper
3 T. grated Parmesan cheese

Build a campfire using briquettes and dig a hole in the coals for the Dutch oven. Place sausage in a 12" Dutch oven and set Dutch oven in hole. Cook sausage for 5 to 10 minutes, until evenly browned. Drain pot of grease and transfer sausage to a separate plate. If using links, chop sausage links into pieces. Unroll crescent rolls and line the bottom of Dutch oven with crescent rolls. Sprinkle sausage, diced bell peppers, hash browns, sliced green onions and shredded Cheddar cheese over crescent rolls. In a medium bowl, combine eggs, milk, salt and pepper. Pour mixture evenly over ingredients in Dutch oven. Sprinkle grated Parmesan cheese over egg mixture. Place lid on Dutch oven and set 8 to 10 briquettes on lid. Bake breakfast pizza for 20 to 30 minutes or until eggs are set.

Equipment needed:
matches
briquettes
12" Dutch oven
sharp knife
medium bowl
spoon
measuring spoons

Fruit Filled Breakfast Bread

Makes 8 servings

4 C. Bisquick baking mix
4 tsp. cinnamon
1 C. golden raisins
½ C. chopped dried apples
1 C. shredded coconut
1 C. chopped almonds
1 C. sugar

½ (16 oz.) pkg. Eggbeaters
  dry scrambled egg mix
4 C. shredded carrots
1 C. vegetable oil
2 tsp. vanilla, optional
1¼ C. water

Build a campfire using briquettes and dig a hole in the coals for the Dutch oven. In a large bowl, combine baking mix, cinnamon, golden raisins, chopped dried apples, shredded coconut, chopped almonds, sugar and dry scrambled egg mix. Add shredded carrots, vegetable oil, vanilla and water to dry mixture and mix until a batter forms. Lightly oil Dutch oven and pour batter into Dutch oven. Set Dutch oven in hole. Place lid on Dutch oven and set 15 to 20 briquettes on lid. Bake bread for 25 to 35 minutes, checking after 15 minutes.

Equipment needed:
matches
briquettes
large bowl
spoon
Dutch oven
measuring cup and spoons
vegetable peeler

Quick tip:
Prepare dry mix at home by combining baking mix, cinnamon, golden raisins, chopped dried apples, shredded coconut, chopped almonds, sugar and dry scrambled egg mix. Pack mixture in a ziplock bag until ready to prepare recipe. Shred carrots at home and pack in a separate bag.

Pasta Dogs

Makes 10 servings

2 (6 oz.) pkgs. spaghetti pasta   **1 (28 oz.) jar pasta sauce**
1 pkg. hot dogs

    Build a campfire using briquettes and dig a hole in the coals for the Dutch oven. Fill Dutch oven with water and set Dutch oven in hole. Add spaghetti to pot and bring to a boil. Meanwhile, cut hot dogs into bite-size pieces. When spaghetti is tender, drain Dutch oven and return cooked spaghetti to the pot. Add pasta sauce and hot dog pieces. Mix well and cook over heat until hot dogs are heated throughout.

Equipment needed:
matches
briquettes
Dutch oven
sharp knife
cooking spoon

One Pot Lasagna

Makes 12 servings

2 lbs. lasagna noodles
5 lbs. ground beef
3 lbs. spicy ground sausage
2 (16 oz.) containers cottage cheese

6 eggs
3 (8 oz.) pkgs. shredded mozzarella cheese
1 (28 oz.) jar pasta sauce

Build a campfire using briquettes and dig a hole in the coals for the Dutch oven. Fill a 14" Dutch oven with water and set Dutch oven in hole. Bring water to a boil and add lasagna noodles. Cook until noodles are tender and transfer noodles to a plate. Drain pot. Place ground beef and spicy ground sausage in Dutch oven. Cook ground beef and sausage for 5 to 10 minutes, until evenly browned. Drain pot of grease and transfer ground beef and sausage to a separate plate. In a medium bowl, combine cottage cheese and eggs. Build lasagna by placing layers of meat, cottage cheese mixture, shredded mozzarella cheese and noodles in Dutch oven. Repeat layers until pot is almost full. Pour spaghetti sauce over lasagna and sprinkle remaining shredded cheese on top. Place lid on Dutch oven and set 10 to 12 briquettes on lid. Cook over heat for about 45 minutes.

Equipment needed:
matches
briquettes
14" Dutch oven
cooking spoon
2 plates
medium bowl

Quick tip:
Cook ground beef and ground sausage at home and pack in an airtight container. Place in cooler until ready to prepare recipe.

Campsketti

Makes 10 servings

½ lb. lean ground beef
1 medium onion, chopped
1 (4 oz.) can mushrooms, drained, optional
1 (14 oz.) can chicken broth
1 (6 oz.) can tomato paste
1¾ C. water

¼ tsp. pepper
½ tsp. dried basil
1 tsp. dried oregano
⅛ tsp. garlic powder
1 (6 oz.) pkg. spaghetti pasta, broken

Build a campfire using briquettes and dig a hole in the coals for the Dutch oven. Place ground beef and chopped onions in Dutch oven and set Dutch oven in hole. Cook ground beef and onions for about 5 minutes, until evenly browned. Drain pot of grease and add drained mushrooms, chicken broth, tomato paste, water, pepper, basil, oregano and garlic powder. Bring mixture to a boil and add broken spaghetti. Cook, stirring frequently, until spaghetti is tender, about 20 minutes.

Equipment needed:
matches
briquettes
Dutch oven
sharp knife
can opener
measuring spoons and cups
cooking spoon

Quick tip:
Prepare seasoning packet at home by combining pepper, dried basil, dried oregano and garlic powder in a ziplock bag.

Coca-Cola Chicken

Makes 8 servings

**8 boneless skinless chicken
 breast halves**
1 (12 oz.) can Coca-Cola
1½ C. ketchup

1 yellow onion, diced
3 cloves garlic, minced
1 T. chili powder

Build a campfire using briquettes and dig a hole in the coals for
the Dutch oven. Place chicken breast halves in a 12″ Dutch oven. Set
Dutch oven in hole. In a large bowl, combine Coca-Cola, ketchup,
diced yellow onion, minced garlic and chili powder. Mix well and
pour mixture over chicken. Place lid on Dutch oven and set 14 to 16
briquettes on lid. Bake chicken for 60 to 75 minutes or until chicken is
cooked throughout.

Equipment needed:
matches
briquettes
12″ Dutch oven
large bowl
spoon
sharp knife
measuring cups and spoons

Chicken Pot Pie

Makes 8 servings

2 large chicken breasts, cooked and cubed

2 (8½ oz.) cans mixed vegetables with potatoes

1 (10¾ oz.) can cream of chicken soup

1 (10¾ oz.) can cream of mushroom soup

1 tube of 10 refrigerated biscuits

Build a campfire using briquettes and dig a hole in the coals for the Dutch oven. Place chicken, mixed vegetables in juice, cream of chicken soup and cream of mushroom soup in Dutch oven and set Dutch oven in hole. Mix well and heat mixture, being careful not to boil. When mixture is warmed throughout, place biscuits on top of chicken mixture. Place lid on Dutch oven and set 14 to 16 briquettes on lid. Heat mixture with biscuits for 15 to 30 minutes, checking biscuits after 15 minutes.

Equipment needed:
matches
briquettes
can opener
Dutch oven
cooking spoon

Quick tip:
Prepare chicken breasts at home and cut into cubes. Pack in an airtight container and place in cooler until ready to prepare recipe.

The Camper's Cobbler

Makes 4 servings

1 (29 oz.) can sliced peaches in syrup
1 (30 oz.) can fruit cocktail in syrup
1 (20 oz.) can crushed pineapple in juice

½ C. instant tapioca
1 (18 oz.) pkg. white cake mix
1 C. brown sugar
½ C. butter or margarine

Build a campfire using briquettes and dig a hole in the coals for the Dutch oven. Line Dutch oven with aluminum foil. Open all cans and add sliced peaches in syrup, fruit cocktail in syrup, crushed pineapple in juice and instant tapioca to Dutch oven. Set Dutch oven in hole. Sprinkle white cake mix over fruit and tapioca and sprinkle brown sugar over cake mix. Dab pieces of butter over brown sugar. Place lid on Dutch oven and set 14 to 16 briquettes on lid. Bake cobbler for 45 to 60 minutes. The cobbler is done when cake mix has absorbed the juices and is no longer dry.

Equipment needed:
matches
briquettes
Dutch oven
aluminum foil
can opener
measuring cups
knife
cooking spoon

Black Forest Cobbler

Makes 4 to 6 servings

1 (12 oz.) can cherry pie filling   **¼ C. chopped walnuts**
1 (18 oz.) pkg. chocolate   **1 or 2 Hershey's chocolate bars**
  cake mix

Build a campfire using briquettes and dig a hole in the coals
for the Dutch oven. Add cherry pie filling to Dutch oven and pour
chocolate cake mix over cherry filling. Add chopped walnuts. Break
Hershey's bars in pieces and sprinkle over walnuts. Do not stir. Place
lid over Dutch oven and set Dutch oven in hole. Cook for about
45 minutes.

Equipment needed:
matches
briquettes
Dutch oven
can opener
cooking spoon

Fruit & Rice Pudding

Makes 2 servings

¾ C. instant brown rice
1½ C. dried assorted fruit
½ C. evaporated milk
1 (8 oz.) can sweetened
  condensed milk

Pinch of nutmeg
Pinch of ground ginger
Pinch of brown sugar
Pinch of cinnamon

Build a campfire using briquettes and dig a hole in the coals for the Dutch oven. Add 2½ cups water to Dutch oven and bring to a boil. Set Dutch oven in hole and add instant brown rice and dried fruit. Cook until fruit is tender and rice is softened, about 8 to 10 minutes. Add evaporated milk, sweetened condensed milk, nutmeg, ground ginger, brown sugar and cinnamon. Mix well and heat for a few more minutes.

Equipment needed:
matches
briquettes
Dutch oven
measuring cups
can opener
cooking spoon

Quick tip:
Prepare dry mix at home by combining evaporated milk, nutmeg, ground ginger, brown sugar and cinnamon. Pack mixture in a ziplock bag until ready to prepare recipe.

Caramel Apple Crisp

Makes 16 servings

2 (12 oz.) cans apple pie filling
2 tsp. cinnamon
¾ tsp. nutmeg
¼ tsp. ground cloves
¾ tsp. salt
1 (12 oz.) jar caramel sauce

2 C. brown sugar
2 C. flour
1 C. instant oatmeal
½ C. chopped walnuts
1 C. butter, melted

Build a campfire using briquettes and dig a hole in the coals for the Dutch oven. Grease a 12" Dutch oven and add apple pie filling. Sprinkle cinnamon, nutmeg, ground cloves and salt over pie filling and mix well. Pour caramel sauce over apple mixture. In a medium bowl, combine brown sugar, flour, instant oatmeal, chopped walnuts and melted butter. Stir mixture with a fork until coarse crumbs form. Sprinkle topping evenly over apple mixture. Set Dutch oven in hole. Place lid on Dutch oven and set 10 to 12 briquettes on lid. Bake apple crisp for about 60 minutes.

Equipment needed:
matches
briquettes
12" Dutch oven
can opener
measuring spoons
medium bowl
cooking spoon

Quick tip:
Prepare dry mixes at home by combining cinnamon, nutmeg, ground cloves and salt. In a separate bowl, combine brown sugar, flour, instant oatmeal and chopped walnuts. Pack mixes in separate ziplock bags until ready to prepare recipe.

On the Grill

Stuffed Mushrooms

Makes 8 to 10 servings

1 (8 oz.) pkg. fresh mushrooms	1 pkg. dry onion soup mix
2 links fully cooked pork sausage	1 to 2 T. shredded mozzarella cheese

Cover the grate of the grill with aluminum foil. Preheat grill or place grilling grate over campfire. Clean mushrooms and twist off caps. Cut cooked pork sausage into small pieces. In a medium bowl, combine dry onion soup mix and pork sausage. Stuff mushroom caps with a generous amount of sausage mixture. Place stuffed mushrooms, cap side down, on aluminum foil on grill. Cook mushrooms over grill for about 15 to 25 minutes. If desired, top stuffed mushrooms with a bit of shredded mozzarella cheese during last few minutes of grilling time. Cook until cheese is melted.

Equipment needed:
matches
aluminum foil
sharp knife
medium bowl
spoon

Quick tip:
Cook pork sausage links at home. Cut into small pieces and mix with dry onion soup mix. Pack mixture in an airtight container and place in cooler until ready to prepare recipe.

Potato Wedges

Makes 3 to 4 servings

2 to 3 large potatoes, washed and scrubbed
1 T. olive oil

½ tsp. dried thyme
½ tsp. dried oregano
Salt and pepper to taste

Cover the grate of the grill with aluminum foil. Preheat grill or place grilling grate over campfire. Cut potatoes into ⅓" to ½" wedges. Brush potato slices with olive oil and sprinkle with dried thyme and dried oregano. Lay potato wedges over aluminum foil on grill. Sprinkle with salt and pepper to taste. Grill wedges to desired tenderness, turning occasionally.

Equipment needed:
matches
aluminum foil
sharp knife
basting brush

Vegetable Skewers

Makes 4 servings

1 red or green bell pepper, cut into 1" pieces
1 zucchini, cut into ½" pieces
1 yellow squash, cut into ½" pieces

2 (6 oz.) pkgs. large mushrooms
2 T. olive oil
2 T. red wine vinegar

Preheat grill or place grilling grate over campfire. In a heavy duty ziplock bag, place bell pepper pieces, zucchini pieces, yellow squash and mushrooms. Pour olive oil and red wine vinegar in bag and seal. Let vegetables marinate for 15 minutes. Slide vegetables onto 4 long metal skewers. Place vegetable kabobs on hot grate and grill for 5 to 10 minutes, brushing occasionally with remaining olive oil mixture. Grill until vegetables are tender and lightly browned.

Equipment needed:
matches
heavy duty ziplock bag
measuring spoons
sharp knife
4 long metal skewers
basting brush

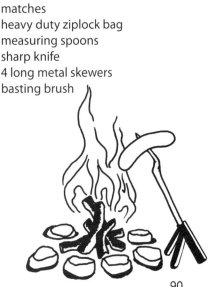

Tender Carrot Slices

Makes 4 servings

4 large carrots, peeled   **2 T. olive oil**

Cover the grate of the grill with aluminum foil. Preheat grill or place grilling grate over campfire. Using a sharp knife, cut carrots in half lengthwise. Brush carrots with olive oil and lay carrots over aluminum foil on grill. Cook carrots to desired tenderness, turning every few minutes.

Equipment needed:
matches
vegetable peeler
sharp knife
basting brush

Corn on the Cob

Makes 4 servings

4 ears of corn
1½ T. butter, melted
½ tsp. ground cumin

¼ tsp. chili powder
1 tsp. fresh chopped cilantro

Preheat grill or place grilling grate over campfire. Pull back husks from ears of corn, leaving the husks attached. Remove 1 strip of husk from the inner side of each ear of corn and set aside. In a small bowl, combine melted butter, ground cumin, chili powder and chopped cilantro. Brush melted butter mixture onto corn. Bring husks up to cover corn and tie husks together with reserved strips of husk. Place corn cobs on the hot grate and grill for 20 to 30 minutes, turning corn occasionally.

Equipment needed:
matches
small bowl
measuring spoons
spoon
basting brush

Quick tip:
To make melted butter mixture, place a small saucepan over grill or fire. Combine butter, ground cumin, chili powder and chopped cilantro in saucepan until melted.

Campfire French Fries

Makes 4 servings

4 potatoes, cut into strips
1 to 2 T. grated Parmesan cheese

Salt and pepper to taste
1 T. butter
2 T. bacon bits

Cover the grate of the grill with aluminum foil. Preheat grill or place grilling grate over campfire. Place potato strips in a heavy duty ziplock bag and add grated Parmesan cheese, salt and pepper. Seal bag and shake until potato strips are covered. Remove potato strips from bag and place on aluminum foil on grill. Dot fries with butter and sprinkle with bacon bits. Cook fries over grill for about 30 to 40 minutes, turning occasionally, until fries are tender.

Equipment needed:
matches
aluminum foil
sharp knife
heavy duty ziplock bag

Grapefruit Egg Custard

Makes 1 serving

1 grapefruit
1 large egg

2 T. milk
Sugar and cinnamon to taste

Preheat grill or place grilling grate over campfire. Using a sharp knife, slice the top from the grapefruit. Spoon pulp from grapefruit cup and eat or discard, setting aside the grapefruit cup. In a small bowl, whisk together egg and milk. Add sugar and cinnamon to taste. Pour egg mixture into grapefruit cup. Place grapefruit cup on grate, propping with coals to stand up straight, if necessary. Cook over fire or grill until egg is set. Carefully remove grapefruit cup from grill and eat egg directly from grapefruit cup. The grapefruit gives the egg an interesting flavor.

Equipment needed:
matches
sharp knife
spoon
small bowl
measuring spoons
fork

Quick tip:
Prepare cinnamon and sugar mixture at home by combining ½ tablespoon sugar and ¼ teaspoon cinnamon. Pack in an airtight container until ready to prepare recipe.

Classic Chicken

Makes 6 servings

1 (3½ lbs.) whole frying chicken, quartered
¼ C. lemon juice
¼ C. olive oil
2 T. soy sauce

2 large cloves garlic, minced
½ tsp. sugar
½ tsp. ground cumin
¼ tsp. pepper

Rinse chicken under running water and pat dry with paper towels. In a heavy duty extra large ziplock bag combine lemon juice, olive oil, soy sauce, minced garlic, sugar, ground cumin and pepper. Place chicken in bag and seal. Let chicken marinate in a cooler filled with ice for 1 hour or overnight. Preheat grill or place grilling grate over campfire. Remove chicken pieces from bag. Place chicken on hot grate, skin side down, for about 25 minutes. Turn chicken pieces and cook for an additional 20 to 25 minutes or until the juices run clear and chicken is cooked throughout.

Equipment needed:
paper towels
heavy duty extra large ziplock bag
measuring spoons
cooler with ice
matches

Quick tip:
Prepare marinade at home and place chicken in bag with marinade. Pack marinating chicken in cooler with ice until ready to prepare recipe.

Big Ranch Burgers

Makes 4 servings

1 C. sliced onions	1 T. butter or margarine
⅓ C. sliced green bell pepper strips	3 T. A.1. steak sauce
⅓ C. sliced red bell pepper strips	2 tsp. prepared horseradish
	1 lb. ground beef
	4 hamburger buns, split

Preheat grill or place grilling grate over campfire. Place a skillet on the hot grate and cook sliced onions, green bell pepper strips and red bell pepper strips in butter, heating until vegetables are tender but crisp. Stir in steak sauce and horseradish. Shape ground beef into 4 burgers and place burgers on hot grate. Cook burgers over grill for 8 to 10 minutes, turning once, until thoroughly cooked to desired doneness. Remove burgers from grate and place on buns. Top each burger with ¼ cup of the cooked onions and peppers.

Equipment needed:
matches
sharp knife
medium skillet
measuring spoons
spoon

Beer Brat Sticks

Makes 6 servings

5 beer bratwursts, cut into 1" pieces

1 zucchini, cut into 1" pieces

1 yellow squash, cut into 1" pieces

1 red onion, cut into 1" pieces

1 green bell pepper, cut into 1" pieces

1 red bell pepper, cut into 1" pieces

2 C. fresh button mushrooms

2 C. barbecue sauce

Preheat grill or place grilling grate over campfire. Soak 6 (10") wooden skewers in water for 30 minutes. Slide bratwurst pieces, zucchini pieces, squash pieces, onion pieces, bell pepper pieces and mushrooms onto skewers. Place skewers on hot grate and grill for 12 to 15 minutes, brushing often with the barbecue sauce. Grill kabobs until bratwurst pieces are cooked throughout.

Equipment needed:
matches
6 wooden skewers
sharp knife
measuring cups
basting brush

Stuffed Frankfurters

Makes 8 servings

8 frankfurters   **8 slices bacon**
**1 (6 oz.) pkg. stuffing mix,
    prepared**

Preheat grill or place grilling grate over campfire. Using a knife, cut
a lengthwise slit in each frankfurter. Stuff frankfurters with prepared
stuffing. Wrap one slice of bacon around each frankfurter, holding
the stuffing inside. Secure with toothpicks. Place frankfurters over
grill and cook until bacon reaches desired crispness and frankfurters
reach desired doneness. Remove toothpicks before serving.

Equipment needed:
matches
knife
spoon
toothpicks
Quick tip:
Prepare stuffing at home and pack in an airtight container. Place
in cooler until ready to prepare recipe.

Beer Can Chicken

Makes 4 to 6 servings

1 (4 to 5 lbs.) whole chicken	**¾ tsp. pepper**
¾ tsp. kosher salt	**¾ tsp. paprika**
¾ tsp. sugar	**1 (12 oz.) can beer**

Preheat grill or place grilling grate over campfire. Remove and discard fat from inside the body cavity of the chicken. Remove giblets and rinse chicken, inside and out, under cool running water. Drain chicken and pat dry with paper towels. In a small bowl, combine kosher salt, sugar, pepper and paprika. Mix well. Sprinkle 1 tablespoon of the rub inside the body cavity and spread the remaining rub over the outside of the chicken. Open beer can and, using a can opener, poke 6 or 7 holes in the top of the can. Drink or pour out 1" of beer from the can. Holding the chicken upright, insert beer can into body cavity of chicken. Cover tips of the chicken legs with aluminum foil and stand chicken up on beer can over center of hot grate. Spread out legs of chicken to form a tripod. Cook chicken until meat is tender, about 2 hours, and internal temperature of chicken reaches 160°. Carefully remove can from chicken, being careful not to spill the hot beer. To serve, carve chicken from the bone.

Equipment needed:
matches
paper towels
small bowl
measuring spoons
can opener
aluminum foil
meat thermometer
sharp knife

Quick tip:
Prepare seasoning rub at home and pack in an airtight container until ready to prepare recipe.

Cheese-Stuffed Brats

Makes 5 servings

5 fully cooked bratwurst
¼ C. shredded Monterey
  Jack cheese
2 green onions, thinly sliced
5 slices bacon

5 hot dog buns or French-style
  rolls, halved lengthwise
Ketchup, mustard and/or
  relish, optional

Preheat grill or place grilling grate over campfire. Using a knife, cut a lengthwise slit, about ½" deep, in each bratwurst. Stuff each bratwurst with some of the shredded Monterey Jack cheese and green onion slices. Wrap one slice of bacon around each bratwurst, holding the cheese inside. Secure with toothpicks. Place bratwurst, cheese side up, over grill and cook until bacon reaches desired crispness and bratwurst reach desired doneness, about 5 to 10 minutes. Remove toothpicks from bratwurst and place each bratwurst on 1 hot dog bun. If desired, garnish with ketchup, mustard and/or relish.

Equipment needed:
matches
sharp knife
spoon
toothpicks

Teriyaki-Chicken Kabobs

Makes 6 servings

4 boneless, skinless chicken breast halves, cut into 1" cubes

2 medium zucchini, cut into ½" thick slices

1 green bell pepper, cut into 1" squares

1 small red onion, cut into ½" cubes

1 C. teriyaki sauce, divided

½ tsp. Lawry's seasoned pepper

¼ tsp. garlic powder

In a heavy duty ziplock bag, place chicken cubes, zucchini slices, green bell pepper squares and red onion cubes. Pour ¾ cup teriyaki sauce into bag and seal. Let chicken and vegetables marinate in a cooler with ice for 30 minutes. Preheat grill or place grilling grate over campfire. Slide marinated chicken and vegetables onto long metal skewers. Sprinkle skewers with Lawry's seasoned pepper and garlic powder. Place skewers on the hot grate and grill kabobs for 10 to 15 minutes or until chicken is cooked throughout. Baste kabobs with remaining ¼ cup teriyaki sauce, however, avoid basting during last 5 minutes of grilling time.

Equipment needed:
heavy duty ziplock bag
cooler with ice
matches
long metal skewers
basting brush

Fireside Pizza

Makes 4 to 6 servings

1 (13 or 14 oz.) tube prepared
  pizza crust
1 (14½ oz.) can pizza sauce
1 (8 oz.) pkg. shredded cheese,
  any kind

Pizza toppings, such as
  pepperoni slices, tomatoes,
  mushrooms,
green peppers, etc.

Cover the grate of the grill with aluminum foil. Preheat grill or place grilling grate over campfire. Place prepared pizza crust on aluminum foil on grill. Top crust with pizza sauce, shredded cheese and pizza toppings of choice. Cook pizza until cheese is melted.

Equipment needed:
matches
aluminum foil
can opener
spoon
pizza cutter or scissors

Honey Garlic Pork Chops

Makes 4 servings

¼ C. lemon juice
¼ C. honey
2 T. soy sauce
1 T. dry sherry

2 cloves garlic, minced
4 (4 oz.) boneless lean
  pork chops

In a heavy duty ziplock bag, combine lemon juice, honey, soy sauce, dry sherry and minced garlic. Place pork chops in bag and seal. Let pork chops marinate in a cooler filled with ice for 4 hours or overnight. Preheat grill or place grilling grate over campfire. Remove pork chops from bag and place pork chops on hot grate. Grill pork chops for 12 to 15 minutes, turning once, until pork chops reach an internal temperature of 155° to 160°.

Equipment needed:
heavy duty ziplock bag
measuring spoons
cooler with ice
matches
meat thermometer

Quick tip:
Prepare marinade at home and place pork chops in bag with marinade. Pack marinating pork chops in cooler with ice until ready to prepare recipe.

Carne Asada

Makes 4 servings

4 (¾" thick) beef rib eye steaks, trimmed
2 T. fresh lime juice
4 (6") flour tortillas

1 C. shredded Colby and Monterey Jack cheese, divided
Salsa

Preheat grill or place grilling grate over campfire. Sprinkle half of the lime juice onto one side of each steak and rub into surface. Turn steaks and repeat with remaining lime juice. Wrap tortillas in aluminum foil. Place steaks on hot grate and grill for 12 to 15 minutes, turning once, or until steaks reach desired doneness. During last 5 minutes of cooking time, place aluminum-wrapped tortillas on outer edge of grate, turning once. Top each steak with ¼ cup shredded cheese and grill for an additional 1 or 2 minutes. Remove steaks from grill and top each steak with salsa. Serve steaks with heated tortillas on the side.

Equipment needed:
matches
sharp knife
aluminum foil
spoon

The All-American Burger

Makes 4 servings

1½ lbs. ground beef	1 tsp. salt
2 tsp. Worcestershire sauce	1 tsp. pepper
2 T. fresh chopped parsley	4 hamburger buns, split
2 tsp. onion powder	Ketchup, mustard, chopped
1 tsp. garlic powder	onions, relish, optional

Preheat grill or place grilling grate over campfire. In a medium bowl, combine ground beef, Worcestershire sauce, chopped parsley, onion powder, garlic powder, salt and pepper. Mix lightly but thoroughly. Shape mixture into four burgers, each about ½" thick. Place burgers on hot grate. Cook burgers over grill for 8 to 10 minutes, turning once, until thoroughly cooked to desired doneness. Remove burgers from grate and place burgers on buns. If desired, garnish burgers with ketchup, mustard, chopped onions and/or relish.

Equipment needed:
matches
medium bowl
measuring spoons
spoon

Quick tip:
Prepare burger mix at home by combining chopped parsley, onion powder, garlic powder, salt and pepper. Pack mixture in an airtight container until ready to prepare recipe. Add ground beef and Worcestershire sauce at campsite.

Southwest Chicken

Makes 4 servings

2 T. olive oil
1 clove garlic, pressed
1 tsp. chili powder
1 tsp. ground cumin

1 tsp. dried oregano
½ tsp. salt
1 lb. skinless boneless chicken
   breast halves or thighs

Preheat grill or place grilling grate over campfire. In a small bowl, combine olive oil, pressed garlic, chili powder, ground cumin, dried oregano and salt. Brush mixture over both sides of chicken breasts or thighs. Place chicken on hot grate and cook over grill for 8 to 10 minutes, turning once, until chicken is cooked throughout.

Equipment needed:
matches
small bowl
measuring spoons
basting brush
sharp knife

Quick tip:
Prepare basting sauce at home and pack in an airtight container. Place in cooler until ready to prepare recipe.

Salmon on the Barbie

Makes 4 servings

4 salmon steaks,
(¾" to 1" thick)
3 T. lemon juice

2 T. soy sauce
Salt and pepper to taste
½ C. barbecue sauce

Preheat grill or place grilling grate over campfire. Rinse salmon steaks under running water and pat dry with paper towels. In a heavy duty ziplock bag, combine lemon juice and soy sauce. Place salmon steaks in bag and let marinate for no more than 15 minutes. Remove salmon from bag and season lightly with salt and pepper. Place salmon steaks on hot grate and cook for 10 to 14 minutes. Halfway through grilling time, brush salmon steaks with barbecue sauce, turn and continue grilling. Salmon is done when it flakes easily with a fork. Remove salmon from grate and brush with additional barbecue sauce.

Equipment needed:
matches
paper towels
heavy duty ziplock bag
measuring spoons
basting brush
fork

Our Favorite Cheddar Burger

Makes 4 servings

1 lb. ground beef
⅓ C. steak sauce, divided
4 (1 oz.) slices Cheddar cheese
1 medium onion, cut into strips
1 medium green or red bell
   pepper, cut into strips

1 T. butter or margarine
4 hamburger buns, split
4 slices tomato

Preheat grill or place grilling grate over campfire. In a medium bowl, combine ground beef and 3 tablespoons steak sauce. Mix lightly but thoroughly. Divide mixture into 4 equal parts. Shape each part into a burger, enclosing one slice of Cheddar cheese inside each burger and set aside. Place a skillet on the hot grate and cook onions and bell pepper strips in butter, heating until vegetables are tender. Stir in remaining steak sauce and keep warm. Place burgers on hot grate. Cook burgers over grill for 8 to 10 minutes, turning once, until thoroughly cooked to desired doneness. Remove burgers from grate and place burgers on buns. Top each burger with a tomato slice and some of the cooked onions and peppers.

Equipment needed:
matches
medium bowl
measuring spoons
sharp knife
medium skillet
spoon

Tropical Shrimp Skewers

Makes 2 servings

¼ C. barbecue sauce
2 T. pineapple or orange juice
2 nectarines
10 oz. medium shrimp, peeled
   and deveined

1 yellow onion, cut
   into wedges

Preheat grill or place grilling grate over campfire. In a medium bowl, combine barbecue sauce and pineapple juice and set aside. Cut each nectarine into 6 wedges. Slide shrimp, nectarines and onion wedges onto 4 long metal skewers. Place skewers on hot grate and grill for 4 to 5 minutes, brushing often with the barbecue sauce mixture. Shrimp are done when they turn opaque.

Equipment needed:
matches
medium bowl
measuring spoons
spoon
sharp knife
long metal skewers
basting brush

Cowboy Kabobs

Makes 4 servings

½ C. spicy steak sauce
½ C. barbecue sauce
2½ tsp. prepared horseradish
1 (1½ lb.) beef top round steak, cut into ½" thick strips
4 medium red skin potatoes, cut into wedges

1 medium onion, cut into wedges
⅓ C. red bell pepper strips
⅓ C. green bell pepper strips
⅓ C. yellow bell pepper strips

Soak 8 (10") wooden skewers in water for 30 minutes. In a medium bowl, combine steak sauce, barbecue sauce and horseradish. In a heavy duty ziplock bag, combine steak strips and vegetables. Pour in steak sauce mixture and seal. Let steak and vegetables marinate in a cooler filled with ice for 1 hour. Preheat grill or place grilling grate over campfire. Alternating, slide steak strips (like an accordion), potato wedges, onion wedges and bell pepper strips onto skewers. Place skewers on hot grate and grill for 6 to 10 minutes or until steak pieces reach desired doneness.

Equipment needed:
8 wooden skewers
medium bowl
spoon
measuring cups
sharp knife
heavy duty ziplock bag
cooler with ice
matches

Chocolate Peanut Butter Cups

Makes 4 servings

4 miniature graham cracker pie crusts

1 ripe banana

12 miniature Reeses peanut butter cups

1 pkg. miniature marshmallows

Preheat grill or place grilling grate over campfire. Place miniature graham cracker pie crusts in a 9 x 13" metal baking dish. Slice banana into pieces. Layer 3 to 4 banana slices in each pie crust. Place 3 miniature peanut butter cups over top of bananas in each crust. Sprinkle several miniature marshmallows over peanut butter cups in each pie crust. Cover baking dish with aluminum foil. Place baking dish over grill for 10 to 15 minutes. Using a hot pad or oven mitt, carefully remove pie crusts from baking dish.

Equipment needed:
matches
9 x 13" metal baking dish
knife
aluminum foil
hot pad or oven mitt

Toasted Pesto Rounds

Makes 12 servings

¼ C. fresh chopped basil or dill
¼ C. grated Parmesan cheese
1 clove garlic, minced
3 T. mayonnaise
1 loaf French bread, cut into
   ¼" thick slices

4 tsp. chopped tomato
1 green onion, sliced
Pepper to taste

Preheat grill or place grilling grate over campfire. In a small bowl, combine chopped basil, grated Parmesan cheese, minced garlic and mayonnaise. Mix well. Lay French bread slices on hot grate for about 1 to 2 minutes, until lightly toasted. Turn slices over and spread an even amount of the mayonnaise mixture over one side of each slice of bread. Top each slice with some of the chopped tomato and sliced green onions. Grill for an additional minute, until bread slices are lightly browned. Season with pepper to taste.

Equipment needed:
matches
small bowl
spoon
sharp knife

Before You Leave Home

Rocky Trail Hiking Mix

Makes 5 ½ cups

3 C. frosted mini wheat squares	½ C. pumpkin seeds, shelled
½ C. raisins or currants	½ C. dried mixed fruit
½ C. sunflower seeds, shelled	½ C. M&M's
	½ tsp. salt, optional

In a large bowl, combine frosted mini wheat squares, raisins, sunflower seeds, pumpkin squares, dried mixed fruit, M&M's and salt. Toss gently with hands until evenly incorporated. Pack mixture in a large ziplock bag.

Equipment needed:
large bowl
measuring cups and spoons
large ziplock bag

Cran-GORP

Makes 5 cups

½ C. mixed nuts
½ C. macadamia nuts
1 C. dried cranberries
  or craisins

1 C. M&M's
1 C. sunflower seeds, shelled

In a large bowl, combine mixed nuts, macadamia nuts, dried cranberries, M&M's and sunflower seeds. Toss gently with hands until evenly incorporated. Pack mixture in a large ziplock bag.

Equipment needed:
large bowl
measuring cups
spoon
large ziplock bag

Camping Crunch

Makes 10 cups

7 C. crispy rice cereal	½ tsp. garlic salt
1 C. mini pretzel sticks	½ tsp. onion salt
1 C. bite-size cheese crackers	2½ tsp. lemon juice
1 C. cashews or peanuts	5 tsp. Worcestershire sauce
¼ C. margarine, melted	

Preheat oven to 450°. In a large bowl, combine crispy rice cereal, mini pretzel sticks, cheese crackers and cashews. Mix well with hands. Place butter in a glass measuring cup. Melt butter in microwave and pour over dry ingredients. Sprinkle with garlic salt, onion salt, lemon juice and Worcestershire sauce and mix well. Spread mixture evenly into an 11 x 17" jellyroll pan. Bake mixture in oven for 45 to 60 minutes, stirring after every 15 minutes. Remove pan from oven and spread mixture onto paper towels to dry. Pack mixture in a large ziplock bag.

Equipment needed:
oven
large bowl
microwave
glass measuring cup
measuring cups and spoons
11 x 17" jellyroll pan
spoon
paper towels
large ziplock bag

Picnic Pasta Salad

Makes 10 cups

3 C. small pasta shells
1 C. chopped broccoli
1 C. chopped zucchini
1 C. chopped tomatoes
½ C. shredded carrots
½ C. chopped green onions
½ C. chopped radishes

½ C. chopped green bell pepper
¾ C. Italian salad dressing
½ lb. diced cooked chicken or turkey
2 T. grated Parmesan cheese

Fill a medium pot with water. Bring water to a boil over high heat. Add pasta shells and cook until tender. Drain pasta and cool under cold running water. In a large bowl, combine drained pasta, chopped broccoli, chopped zucchini, chopped tomatoes, shredded carrots, chopped green onions, chopped radishes and chopped green bell pepper. Pour salad dressing over ingredients and add diced cooked chicken and grated Parmesan cheese. Mix all together until evenly incorporated. Pack mixture in an airtight container in a cooler with ice.

Equipment needed:
medium pot
stovetop
colander
large bowl
spoon
sharp knife
large airtight container
cooler with ice

Banana Chips

Makes 2 to 4 servings

2 to 3 ripe bananas

Preheat oven to 150°. Peel and slice bananas into thin rounds. Spray a baking sheet with non-stick cooking spray. Spread banana slices into a single layer onto baking sheet. Bake in oven for 4 hours, turning banana slices over with a fork after 2 hours. Banana chips are done when they are hard and unbendable. Let chips cool on a wire rack and store in a ziplock bag.

Equipment needed:
oven
sharp knife
baking sheet
non-stick cooking spray
hot pad or oven mitt
fork
wire rack
ziplock bag

Café Bavarian Mint Mix

Makes 8 servings

¼ C. powdered creamer
⅓ C. sugar
¼ C. instant coffee granules

2 T. cocoa powder
2 hard mint candies, crushed

In a medium bowl, combine powdered creamer, sugar, instant coffee granules, cocoa powder and crushed mint candies. Toss gently with hands until evenly incorporated. Pack mixture in a large ziplock bag. At campsite, mix 2 tablespoons coffee mixture with 1 to 1½ cups hot water.

Equipment needed:
medium bowl
spoon
large ziplock bag

Swiss Mocha Mix

Makes 6 servings

6 T. powdered milk
3 T. instant coffee granules

3 T. sugar
1¼ tsp. cocoa powder

In a medium bowl, combine powdered milk, instant coffee granules, sugar and cocoa powder. Toss gently with hands until evenly incorporated. Pack mixture in a large ziplock bag. At campsite, mix 2 tablespoons coffee mixture with 1 to 1½ cups hot water.

Equipment needed:
medium bowl
spoon
large ziplock bag

Index

In a Skillet

Before You Leave Home